The Negro Leagues

by Michael Burgan

Content Adviser: Bob Kendrick, Director of Marketing,
Negro Leagues Baseball Museum,
Kansas City, Missouri

Reading Adviser: Rosemary G. Palmer, Ph.D.,
Department of Literacy,
College of Education, Boise State University

Compass Point Books ◈ Minneapolis, Minnesota

Compass Point Books
3109 West 50th Street, #115
Minneapolis, MN 55410

On the cover: Ted "Double Duty" Radcliffe of the West tagged out the East's hard-hitting Josh Gibson at home plate during the East-West Game in 1944 at Chicago's Comiskey Park.

Photographs ©: Bettmann/Corbis, cover; Prints Old and Rare, back cover (far left); Library of Congress, back cover, 14; AP Images/Matty Zimmerman, 4; Mark Rucker/Transcendental Graphics/Getty Images, 6, 12, 13, 16, 24, 25; National Baseball Hall of Fame Library/MLB Photos via Getty Images, 7, 17, 20, 27; AP Images, 8, 34, 36, 38; North Wind Picture Archives, 10; Diamond Images/Getty Images, 18; The Granger Collection, New York, 22, 28, 30; George Skadding/Time & Life Pictures/Getty Images, 33; General Research & Reference Division, Schomburg Center for Research in Black Culture, The New York Public Library, Astor, Lenox and Tilden Foundations, 39; AP Images/Eric Risberg, 40; AP Images/Charlie Riedel, 41.

 This book was manufactured with paper containing at least 10 percent post-consumer waste.

Managing Editor: Catherine Neitge
Page Production: Lori Bye
Photo Researcher: Eric Gohl
Cartographer: Mapping Specialists
Library Consultant: Kathleen Baxter

Creative Director: Keith Griffin
Editorial Director: Nick Healy

Library of Congress Cataloging-in-Publication Data
Burgan, Michael.
  The Negro leagues / by Michael Burgan.
    p. cm.
  Includes index.
  ISBN 978-0-7565-3354-0 (library binding)
1. Negro leagues—History—Juvenile literature. 2. African American baseball players—Juvenile literature. 3. Baseball—United States—History—Juvenile literature. I. Title.
  GV875.A1B87 2008
  796.357'640973—dc22   2007033091

Visit Compass Point Books on the Internet at *www.compasspointbooks.com*
or e-mail your request to *custserv@compasspointbooks.com*

TABLE OF CONTENTS

BASEBALL'S COLOR LINE

On the mound, a tall, skinny pitcher began to throw. With arms and legs winding up and then whipping forward, he released the baseball. The batter could only wave at a pitch that was almost too fast to see. Leroy "Satchel" Paige chalked up another strikeout.

The Kansas City Monarchs won four Negro American League pennants in a row and one black World Series behind the pitching of Leroy "Satchel" Paige.

Nearly 18,000 fans watched Paige work against star pitcher Dizzy Dean on this November night in 1934. Both men were the leaders of barnstorming teams—baseball teams that traveled around the country appearing in exhibition games. The two teams had traveled to California to play during the fall. Dean had just won 30 regular-season games for the St. Louis Cardinals. He then won two more in the World Series, leading the Cardinals to the championship. Dean had had one of the greatest seasons ever and was named the National League's Most Valuable Player.

But Dean's team of major league stars could not beat Paige that night. In a game that went 13 innings, Paige threw 17 strikeouts, leading his team to a 1-0 win.

To many baseball experts, Satchel Paige was the greatest pitcher of all time. But Paige did not play in the majors that season, or for many seasons in his long career. He would not reach the big leagues until 1948, when he was 42 years old. (But Paige's age has always been in question. Some baseball experts believe Paige was more than 50 years

Powerful home run hitter Josh Gibson died a few months before baseball's color line was broken.

old when he made it to the big leagues.)

Paige was an African-American, and until after World War II, Major League Baseball had what was called the color line. Only whites were allowed to play for the major league teams and for the minor league teams that helped train their players. Great black athletes such as Paige and the hard-hitting catcher Josh Gibson instead played in the Negro Leagues.

The first successful professional league for blacks was established in 1920. It fell on hard economic times and disbanded. But by 1934, the year of Paige's classic game against Dean, it was back. The Negro National League (NNL) had six teams. Other professional black teams played both NNL teams and semi-pro teams. Another league, the Negro American League, formed in 1937, and the two Negro Leagues had their own all-star game and World Series.

Baseball's color line reflected the relations between

The 1935 Pittsburgh Crawfords, one of the best teams in the history of the leagues

Two of the best, Satchel Paige (left) and Dizzy Dean, talked before a 1942 game.

black and white Americans of the time. The United States was a segregated nation, especially in the South. Blacks could not sit with whites in movie theaters or some major league ballparks. Blacks went to separate hospitals, ate in separate restaurants, and sent their children to all-black schools.

The U.S. Supreme Court, the country's most powerful court, had paved the way for this separation in 1896. In a case called *Plessy v. Ferguson*, the court said segregation was legal. The only condition was that the buildings and services used by African-Americans had to be as good as the ones for whites. In reality African-Americans rarely received equal treatment.

Baseball was a prime example. Dizzy Dean summed up what some baseball experts of the day believed: "It's too bad those colored boys don't play in the big leagues because they sure got some great ball players." Decades later, more white Americans realized Dean had been right. Many great players of the Negro Leagues slowly received the fame they deserved. But that praise came long after they had stopped playing the game they loved.

THE EARLY YEARS

Segregation and the color line were products of the racism many whites felt toward African-Americans. It had started with the enslavement of blacks, which began when the nation was just forming. Wealthy whites bought Africans who had been taken from their homes to the New World and enslaved. The slaves were treated not as people but

Enslaved children worked in the sugarcane fields of the South.

10

as property. During the 19th century, the economy of the Southern states was tied to growing cotton, which required many workers in the fields. Owning slaves was cheaper than paying workers to do this hot, difficult work.

Sometimes young white boys and black slaves played together. Former slaves later recalled their experiences playing baseball. One told a government researcher, "We never had to buy a ball or bat. … The white boys bought them."

In 1845, a type of baseball similar to today's game was first played in Hoboken, New Jersey, just outside New York City. That area also saw the first known game between two all-black teams. In 1859, the Henson Base Ball Club, of Queens, New York, defeated the Weeksville Unknowns of Brooklyn, New York.

Slavery ended in the United States after the North defeated the South in the Civil War in 1865. In the years that followed, black teams sometimes played white teams. In 1870, an African-American team from New York called the Mutuals traveled across the East. The Mutuals mostly played other black teams, though it beat a team of local white all-stars in Rochester, New York. A newspaper reported, "A larger gathering was, perhaps, never before assembled on the commons to witness a game of ball." In the following years, other black teams barnstormed the nation.

During the 1870s, Bud Fowler became the first African-American known to have played professionally for a white club. The first known black player on a major

The 1890 Baltimore Blues were the "Colored Champions of Maryland."

Moses Fleetwood Walker (back row, far right) retired after playing the 1888–1889 season with the Syracuse Stars. He also played in Toledo and Newark.

league team was Moses Fleetwood Walker. He played for Toledo, which in 1884 joined one of the first pro leagues, the American Association. In 1907, African-American ballplayer and historian Sol White wrote about the first black players. According to his research, "In 1887, no less than 20 colored players [were] scattered among the different smaller leagues of the country."

THE SEPARATION BEGINS

By the 1890s, however, the color line had come to baseball. Sol White placed much of the blame on Adrian "Cap" Anson, the captain of the National League team in Chicago (now called the Cubs). Anson had strong racist views and refused to play against African-Americans. In other cities, black players heard insults from their teammates and the fans. By the end of the century, Anson and other baseball leaders had established a "gentleman's agreement" that kept black players from being hired by

Adrian "Cap" Anson maintained his racist views during the 27 years he played professional baseball.

white teams. Blacks no longer played in the major leagues or for the top minor league teams.

Although blacks could not play in white leagues, they still played against white semipro teams. They also played each other. In the early 1900s, the best black teams included the Philadelphia Giants and the Brooklyn Royal Giants.

In 1906, four black teams and two white teams formed the International League of Independent Base Ball Clubs. When the season ended, two black teams, the Philadelphia Giants and the Cuban X Giants, played what was called the World's Colored Championship. Philadelphia won this first championship.

The International League was soon followed by the National Association of Colored Baseball Clubs. But the leagues were not as well organized as the major leagues. The number of games played during a season varied, and no one kept detailed records of players' statistics. By 1912, the first two black baseball leagues had failed.

But fans who attended the league games had seen

15

Smokey Joe Williams (1885–1946) is considered one of the best pitchers in all of baseball.

great players, including pitcher Smokey Joe Williams. In the late 1910s, in an exhibition game against a white team from the National League, Williams struck out 20 batters while pitching a no-hitter. Another star pitcher was Andrew "Rube" Foster. Today Foster is remembered more for what he did off the playing field than on it.

While still a player, Foster organized the Chicago American Giants, and the team built up a loyal group of fans. Foster also scheduled games for the team across the country. During the 1910s, other cities in the Midwest—including Kansas City and Indianapolis—developed strong professional black teams. At times white businessmen owned the teams or helped schedule games. They often had more money to invest than blacks, and they did not face prejudice from the white businessmen who owned most baseball parks.

In 1920, Foster and the owners of other professional black teams formed the Negro National League. This league was much more successful than the first two, and Foster is sometimes called the father of black baseball. Three years later, teams based in the eastern United States formed the

Rube Foster earned his nickname when he defeated white Hall of Fame pitcher Rube Waddell in a 1902 exhibition game.

Eastern Colored League. In 1924, the best team from each league played in the first Negro World Series. The Kansas City Monarchs of the NNL beat Philadelphia's Hilldale Giants, five games to four.

17

GOOD TIMES AND BAD TIMES

Most of the teams in the new leagues were based in cities
with large African-American populations. During World
War I (1914–1918), about 500,000 blacks left farming
communities and small towns in the South to take jobs
in northern and Midwestern cities. Chicago saw its black
population more than double, going from 44,000 to 110,000.

Rube Foster (front row, center) and his 1914 Chicago American Giants

New York, Philadelphia, and other cities saw similar increases. This "Great Migration" meant black business owners had more customers. Black baseball team owners hoped it would be the same for them.

The cities with large black populations often had newspapers owned and operated by blacks and written for blacks. A writer for one of these papers, the Kansas City *Call*, said baseball was a "source of interest, pride, and race glory."

The Negro Leagues of the 1920s produced several stars who were as talented as the best white players of the day. They included Oscar Charleston, William Julius "Judy" Johnson, James "Cool Papa" Bell, John Henry "Pop" Lloyd, and Wilber "Bullet Joe" Rogan. Charleston was a great all-around player. Johnson was one of the best fielders in the game. Bell was considered the fastest man in the game and could score from second base on a bunt. Lloyd was excellent at hitting "in the clutch"—when men were on base and his team needed runs. Rogan was mainly a pitcher but was also a great all-around player.

James "Cool Papa" Bell (sliding) is considered the fastest man ever to play baseball.

Despite the talents of these and other players, the two Negro Leagues struggled to survive. Many African-American fans could not afford tickets, so team owners could not make enough money to pay their players and their bills. Even if fans could afford to go to the games, many chose not to. The teams still had trouble gathering and publishing statistics, which many baseball fans enjoyed having. People wanted to know who was the best at a particular position and how their favorite players were doing. Newspapers sometimes failed to print the league results.

In addition, owners often did not punish players who broke the rules. Players would ignore umpires, knowing they would not be fined. One newspaper wrote about a Baltimore Black Sox pitcher who refused to give an umpire the ball: "[He] … told the umpire that if he wanted to see it he might come out and get it." To some, the Negro Leagues did not seem as serious about baseball as the major leagues.

The faltering U.S. economy also affected the Negro Leagues. In 1928, companies began to fire workers. At integrated companies, blacks were often the first workers fired. The next year, the country entered the Great Depression, a worldwide economic downturn that lasted more than 10 years. Millions of people lost their jobs, so even fewer people could afford to go to Negro Leagues games. The Eastern League had already played its last game in 1928, though some of its teams continued as independent barnstormers.

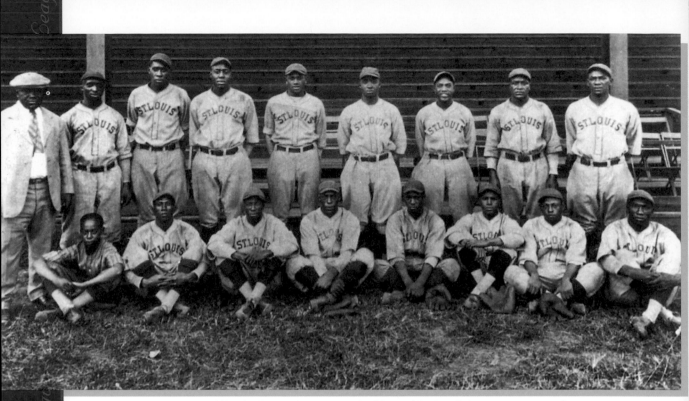

The St. Louis Stars won the Negro National League pennant three times,
including during the league's final season in 1931.

By 1930, the Kansas City Monarchs of the NNL
also saw they could do better as a barnstorming team.
Few whites would watch two black teams play. But the
Monarchs could draw white fans by playing white semipro
teams. The next year, the NNL went out of business.

THE NEW NEGRO LEAGUES

Gus Greenlee, an African-American businessman who owned the Pittsburgh Crawfords, created a new Negro National League in 1933. Several barnstorming teams refused to join. They did not think a new league could make it during the Great Depression. The league struggled, and the owners lost money. But the Negro National League survived.

In 1933, white Major League Baseball held its first All-Star Game. The new NNL decided to have an all-star game, too, calling it the East-West Game. The game was played at Comiskey Park, home of the Chicago White Sox. (Negro League teams often rented stadiums built for white professional teams.) On a rainy September day, about 12,000 fans watched the West All-Stars beat the East, 11-7. Over the next 15 years, the East-West Game became the highlight of the Negro Leagues season. The game made money for the league and sometimes drew more than 50,000 fans.

For its first two seasons, the NNL was centered in the

Josh Gibson slid home safely during an East-West Game at Comiskey Park.

Midwest and western Pennsylvania. Pittsburgh, with the
Crawfords and the Homestead Grays, had most of the great
African-American stars of the era. Cool Papa Bell, Josh
Gibson, Buck Leonard, and Satchel Paige all played in the
city at some point during the 1930s.

For the 1935 season, the NNL added the Brooklyn

Eagles, its first team on the East Coast. Abraham Manley owned the team, but his wife, Effa, played a larger role in running it. One former player for the Eagles remembered that "she was interested in appearances—uniform neat, shoes shined." Effa Manley wanted the NNL and its players to be respected. Her parents were white and part Native American, but she was raised by a black stepfather. She considered herself African-American and believed strongly that blacks should support black-owned businesses. The Negro Leagues, however, still sometimes relied on white businessmen to help arrange their games.

Effa Manley was a strong advocate for her baseball players. She was also active in the civil rights movement.

The NNL also continued to hunt for fans. Many blacks seemed more interested in the African-American boxer Joe Louis than in baseball. Louis was an amateur champion in 1934 and won the world's heavyweight championship three years later. He remained champ until 1949. In 1936, the black sprinter Jesse Owens won four gold medals at the Summer Olympics in Berlin, Germany. He took attention away from black baseball, too.

The league also had some of the problems the first Negro Leagues had experienced. Some teams preferred to play nonleague teams, because they made more money from those games. Star players left teams if they could make more money barnstorming. And some black fans preferred to watch the major leagues. At the end of the 1936 season, a black sportswriter wrote, "The league as a league is a flop."

Despite those problems, a group of team owners formed a new league for the 1937 season. The Negro American League (NAL) featured teams from the Midwest and the South. The NNL was now mostly centered in the

East. All-stars from the two leagues played each other in the East-West Game, but the leagues did not create a World Series until 1942. The two leagues were rivals that competed for the best players.

But the NNL and NAL shared a common problem. The leagues had to worry about foreign teams taking their stars. Some players went to teams in Mexico or the Caribbean. There the players received better pay and faced less racism than they did in the United States. In the Negro Leagues, players could not stay in hotels that served whites. In smaller towns that did not have black hotels, players had to stay with African-American

Buck Leonard (1907–1997) of the Homestead Grays played in a record 11 East-West Games.

Stars of the 1937 Pittsburgh Crawfords, including Satchel Paige (middle row, right), Cool Papa Bell (front row, center), and Josh Gibson (back row, far left) played on a team sponsored by Dominican Republic President Rafael Trujillo (center).

families. The parks where they played sometimes did not have showers.

George Giles played for the Monarchs and several other teams during the 1930s. He said that in one small town, "we set tubs of water out in the sun to get them warm so we could take a bath."

A Change in Attitude

By 1940, the Great Depression finally began to ease. The start of World War II in Europe had sparked the growth of industry in the United States. President Franklin Roosevelt wanted the country to build weapons for Great Britain and other friendly foreign nations. Then, in December 1941, Japan attacked Pearl Harbor in Hawaii, and soon the United States was fighting in both Europe and Asia.

Jobs created by the war sparked another migration of African-Americans from the South. They went to cities with factories that made weapons and military supplies. With the money they made, blacks could now afford to go to more baseball games. Attendance at Negro Leagues games ballooned. About 36,000 fans came to Yankee Stadium in 1942 to watch Satchel Paige and several NNL teams. Also popular were the Ethiopian Clowns, who mixed humor with baseball. They were compared to the Harlem Globetrotters, who blended laughs and athletic talent in basketball.

In 1943, the Negro American League teams made more money than they ever had before. One sportswriter said Negro Leagues baseball was now a "big business," not "merely a sport or a hobby."

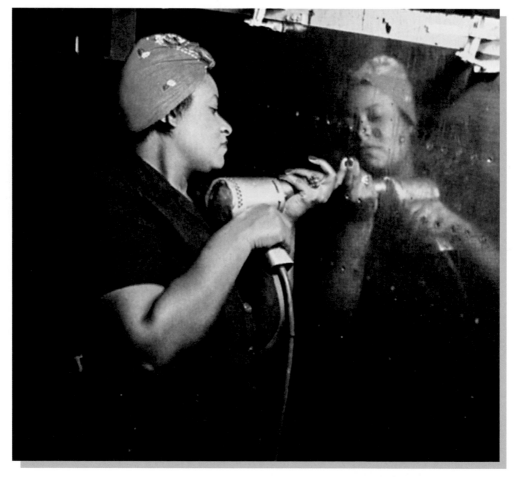

Well-paying jobs became more plentiful during the war years.

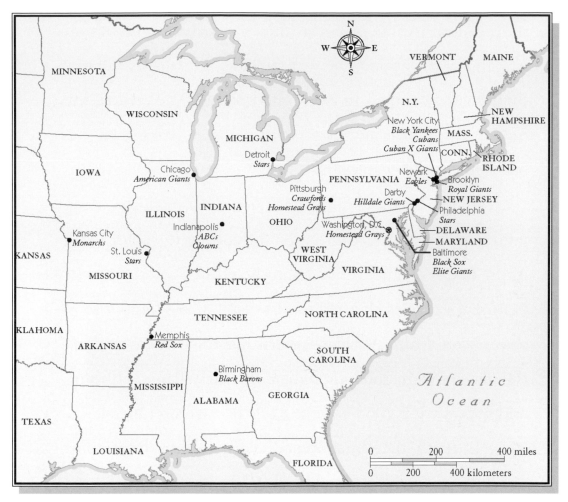

Most Negro Leagues teams were based in the Northeast and Midwest.

World War II also changed the attitudes of many African-Americans and some whites. President Roosevelt said Americans were fighting to defend freedom around the world. Yet at home, most African-Americans lacked the freedom to vote or live as they pleased, because of racism and segregation. The war stirred some blacks to protest their legal treatment in the United States. The civil rights movement, which had its greatest gains 20 years later, was born during the war years.

The push for civil rights affected baseball, too. People who opposed segregation called for ending the color line in the major leagues. Owners in the white American and National Leagues claimed there wasn't a color line. Pro teams would hire African-Americans, the owners said, if the players were good enough. But clearly Paige, Gibson, and others were good enough. Yet they weren't hired.

In truth, the white owners feared losing the support of white fans who disliked blacks. The color line might not have been an official league rule, but no team wanted to be the first to hire a black player.

In 1945, the Brooklyn Dodgers made the first serious effort to break the color line. Branch Rickey, the Dodgers president and part owner, knew there were many talented

The mid-1940s saw the birth of the civil rights movement.

players in the Negro Leagues. He believed they could help
the Dodgers attract black fans. Rickey also knew the color
line was unfair, and he began to look for the perfect player
to break the color line. Before the end of the year, he found
the man he wanted.

33

THE END OF AN ERA

Branch Rickey knew the first African-American in the major leagues would face some hostile white fans. He wanted the first black player to be not just a good ballplayer but also well educated. Rickey found that player on the Kansas City Monarchs of the Negro American League. It was Jackie Robinson.

Jackie Robinson (left) played 10 seasons with Branch Rickey's Brooklyn Dodgers.

Jack Roosevelt Robinson had been a great athlete in high school and college. He ran track and played basketball, football, and baseball. Robinson played just one year with the Monarchs before signing with the Brooklyn Dodgers. He was not the best player to be recruited from the Negro Leagues but he was smart, honorable, and courageous. As one black sportswriter said, Robinson was "the most suitable … he was the right man."

Robinson played one season for the Montreal Royals, a minor league team for the Dodgers. Then, on April 15, 1947, he played his first game in Brooklyn, becoming the first black to play on a modern major league team. The color line was broken.

Other major league teams, however, did not rush to sign Negro Leagues players. Only a handful of black players were in the major leagues during the early years of integrated baseball. These players included Satchel Paige and Larry Doby, who both signed with the Cleveland Indians in 1948. Doby was the first black player in the American League.

During his first full season with the Cleveland Indians of the American League, Larry Doby hit a 400-foot (122-meter) home run to win the fourth game of the 1948 World Series.

Black fans filled the parks wherever Brooklyn and Cleveland played. Slowly, many of these fans stopped going to Negro Leagues games.

The black teams faced other problems. Most had to

pay high fees to rent stadiums from white teams. Difficulty getting the stadiums made it hard to schedule games. Many black newspapers were more interested in reporting on Robinson and the few other black major leaguers.

Also, some old problems had never been solved. Robinson wrote about the bad conditions he had seen in the Negro Leagues. Players had to stay in hotels "of the cheapest kind" and travel long hours on buses between games. Umpires, he said, "are often quite untrained and favor certain teams." The end of the color line in the major leagues just added to the Negro Leagues' troubles.

In 1948, the Negro National League shut down. Over the next 10 years, the Negro American League slowly shrank to just four teams. The last East-West Game was played in 1961. That year about 15 percent of major league players were African-Americans. Some of the stars of the time who had played briefly in the Negro Leagues before joining the majors were Hank Aaron, Willie Mays, and Ernie Banks. All three are now in the Baseball Hall of Fame.

Willie Mays played for the NNL Birmingham Barons before becoming a superstar with the New York Giants.

The last all-black teams were barnstormers. They included the Clowns, who had moved to Indianapolis, and a team led by Satchel Paige. By 1970, even the barnstormers were almost all gone. Few white Americans knew about the stars of the old Negro Leagues. One who did was Ted Williams. The star outfielder of the Boston Red Sox entered the Hall of Fame in 1966. He said then, "I hope that someday, the names of Satchel Paige and Josh Gibson in some way can be added [to the Hall] as a symbol of the great Negro players that are not here only because they were not given a chance." The Hall of Fame soon formed a committee to study the issue of inducting Negro Leagues players. In 1971,

Satchel Paige became the first. He was followed by Josh Gibson, Buck Leonard, and 15 others.

By the end of the 20th century, the history of the Negro Leagues and their players was more widely known. A 1994 documentary, *Baseball*, by filmmaker Ken Burns told the story of the sport, including its African-American players. In 1990, the Negro Leagues Baseball Museum was established. Seven years later it moved to a new home in the 18th and Vine neighborhood near downtown Kansas City. The neighborhood is the city's historic center of African-American culture.

Sol White was involved in black baseball as a player, manager, and historian.

And in February 2006, the Hall of Fame selected a group of 17 African-American players and executives to be inducted. They included Sol White and Frank Grant, who

A young girl walked past a huge photo of the Homestead Grays, part of a tribute to the Negro Leagues during the 2007 All-Star Game.

played before the first Negro Leagues were established. Stars from the Negro Leagues included Biz Mackey, Mule Suttles, and Ray Brown. Also selected was Effa Manley, making her the first woman to enter the Baseball Hall of Fame.

One who didn't make it was John J. "Buck" O'Neil, a Negro Leagues star and the first black hired as a major league coach. To the dismay of baseball fans throughout the country, he missed the cut by one vote.

After the results were announced, O'Neil told his disappointed fans: "Shed no tears for Buck. I couldn't attend Sarasota [Florida] High School. That hurt. I couldn't attend the University of Florida. That hurt. But not going to the

Kansas City Monarchs star and manager Buck O'Neil stood next to a statue of himself at the Negro Leagues Baseball Museum, which he helped establish. In 2007, the Hall of Fame established a Lifetime Achievement Award in his honor.

Hall of Fame, that ain't going to hurt me that much, no. Before, I wouldn't even have a chance. But this time I had that chance. Just keep loving old Buck."

O'Neil, who was a driving force behind the Negro Leagues Baseball Museum and traveled the world to tell the story of black baseball, died several months later at age 94.

Baseball officials cannot change the past, when racism denied talented black athletes a chance at stardom. But they and others work to remind the country of those stars and of the struggle African-Americans have faced to win equality.

41

GLOSSARY

barnstorming—to travel around an area appearing in exhibition sporting events, especially baseball games

civil rights—legal rights guaranteed to every citizen of a country, such as voting and receiving equal treatment

economy—the way a country produces, distributes, and uses its money, goods, natural resources, and services

inducted—brought in as a member, especially in a formal ceremony

integrated—opened to all, regardless of race, such as a place or organization

migration—movement of people from one area to another

prejudice—hatred or unfair treatment of a group of people who belong to a certain race or religion

racism—the belief that one race is better than others

segregated—separated, as in groups of people, based on their race

semipro—athlete who plays for pay on a part-time basis

statistics—numerical facts, such as a baseball player's home runs and batting average

DID YOU KNOW?

- Hall of Famer Josh Gibson was called the "black Babe Ruth." Although detailed records do not exist, it is believed that he led the Negro National League in home runs 10 seasons in a row.

- The Kansas City Monarchs played night games in 1930, five years before the first major league teams did.

- In his first season with the Brooklyn Dodgers, Jackie Robinson batted .297 and led the National League with 29 steals. He was named the league's Rookie of the Year. Two years later, he was the National League's Most Valuable Player. An all-star infielder, Robinson appeared in six World Series. In 1997, Major League Baseball retired his number, 42.

- In 1988, the Pittsburgh Pirates became the first major league club to honor teams from the Negro Leagues. They issued trading cards of players from the Pittsburgh Crawfords and the Homestead Grays. Between them, the two teams finished first in the Negro Leagues 11 straight times.

- In 2006, Buck O'Neil, a star with the Kansas City Monarchs, became the oldest professional player ever, playing in one game at the age of 94. The new home of the John "Buck" O'Neil Education and Research Center is the Kansas City YMCA, where the Negro Leagues were formed.

IMPORTANT DATES

Timeline

1859	First known game between two African-American baseball teams is played in New York
1884	Moses Fleetwood Walker becomes the first black player on a white major league team.
1920	Andrew "Rube" Foster helps form the Negro National League.
1931	The Great Depression and other problems force the NNL to shut down.
1933	Gus Greenlee helps form a new Negro National League; the first East-West Game is played in Chicago.
1937	The Negro American League forms, with teams based in the Midwest and South.
1947	Jackie Robinson plays his first game for the Brooklyn Dodgers, ending the color line.
1971	Satchel Paige becomes the first star from the Negro Leagues to enter the Hall of Fame.
1990	The Negro Leagues Museum established in Kansas City with Buck O'Neil as chairman.
2006	Group of 17 players and executives from the Negro Leagues and earlier black baseball enter the Hall of Fame.

IMPORTANT PEOPLE

ANDREW "RUBE" FOSTER (1879–1930)

Player, manager, and owner of the Chicago American Giants and star pitcher with several other teams; in 1920, he helped form the first Negro National League; Foster was elected to the Baseball Hall of Fame in 1981

GUS GREENLEE (1893–1952)

Owner of the Pittsburgh Crawfords who opened his own ballpark; in 1933, he organized the second Negro National League and established the East-West Game; a powerful politician, he was known as "Mr. Big"

LEROY "SATCHEL" PAIGE (1906–1982)

Negro Leagues pitcher known for his great talent and appeal to fans; he joined the Cleveland Indians in 1948 and helped his team win the American League pennant and the World Series; in 1971, he became the first Negro Leagues star admitted to the Baseball Hall of Fame

MOSES FLEETWOOD WALKER (1857–1924)

First African-American to play for a white major league team, joining the Toledo Blue Stockings in 1883, the year before the team joined a major league; he faced threats from racist players and fans during his career, which ended in 1889; he played college baseball at Oberlin College and the University of Michigan

WANT TO KNOW MORE?

More Books to Read

Landau, Elaine. *The Civil Rights Movement in America.* New York: Children's
Press, 2003.

McKissack, Patricia, and Frederick McKissack. *Satchel Paige: The Best Arm
in Baseball.* Rev. ed. Berkeley Heights, N.J.: Enslow Publishers, 2002.

Winter, Jonah. *Fair Ball! 14 Great Stars from Baseball's Negro Leagues.* New
York: Scholastic Press, 1999.

Wukovits, John F. *Life in the Negro Baseball Leagues.* Detroit: Lucent Books, 2005.

On the Web

For more information on this topic, use FactHound.

1. Go to *www.facthound.com*

2. Type in this book ID: 0756533546

3. Click on the *Fetch It* button.

FactHound will find the best Web sites for you.

On the Road

Negro Leagues Baseball Museum
1616 E. 18th St.
Kansas City, MO 64108
816/221-1920
Exhibits about the stars of the Negro Leagues and their lives during segregation

National Baseball Hall of Fame and Museum
25 Main St.
Cooperstown, NY 13326
607/547-7200
Exhibits on the history of the game and the Negro Leagues players honored by the Hall

Look for more We the People books about this era:

The 19th Amendment
The Berlin Airlift
The Civil Rights Act of 1964
The Dust Bowl
Ellis Island
The Great Depression
The Holocaust Museum
The Korean War
Navajo Code Talkers

Pearl Harbor
The Persian Gulf War
The San Francisco Earthquake of 1906
September 11
The Sinking of the USS Indianapolis
The Statue of Liberty
The Titanic
The Tuskegee Airmen
The Vietnam Veterans Memorial

A complete list of We the People titles is available on our Web site:
www.compasspointbooks.com

INDEX

About the Author

Michael Burgan is a freelance writer of books for children and adults. A history graduate of the University of Connecticut, he has written more than 100 fiction and nonfiction children's books. For adult audiences, he has written news articles, essays, and plays. Michael Burgan is a recipient of an Educational Press Association of America award.